I0004610

Hacking Mastery

A Code Like A Pro Guide
For Computer
Hacking Beginners

INTRODUCTION

Firstly, I want to thank you and congratulate you for downloading the book, Hacking Mastery.

This book contains proven steps and strategies on how to become a hacker and the many ways that you can use your new found hacking skills.

An inescapable fact is that you are able to use your hacking skills for both good and bad. However, it is not recommended that you hack into any system. It is highly illegal!

You should never hack into a system without the administrator's permission. Any hacking that is done without the expressed permission of the system's administrator's permission is strictly illegal and while you may not get caught right away, you can end up spending time in prison or paying some very heavy fines. Any illegal hacking can earn you a sentence of up to twenty years in a federal prison.

Any information in this book is purely for educational purposes!
Thanks again for downloading this book, I hope you enjoy it!

Table of Contents

Introduction

Chapter 1: A Hacker's Mindset

There are five main principals of a hacker's mind that every hacker should think about when they are hacking. If you are looking to begin hacking, you should think of these too.

1.   The world is full of fascinating problems that are just waiting to be solved:

As a hacker you can have a lot of fun (as long as you are doing it legally). But, it does take a lot of effort to be a hacker. And that effort takes a lot of motivation. As a hacker, your motivation is going to come from you solving problems, exercising your intelligence, and even sharpening your skills with each successful hack.

If you are not this way naturally, you will become this way as you learn the ways of being a hacker. If you do not, your energy is going to be sapped by many different distractions such as money and even social approval.

You also need to be able to develop some kind of faith in your own ability to learn. This believe is going to let you know that you can learn how to hack anything you need to, but you do not know everything. If you are able to tackle a problem and learn how to solve just one piece of it, you have learned something and are ready to go on and learn the next thing.

This is you having the faith in yourself to be able to learn how to solve a puzzle one piece at a time.

2.   No problem should ever have to be solved twice: your creative brain is both valuable and a limited resource (because you're the only one of you). Just as they didn't waste any time on re-inventing the wheel, you shouldn't have to go back and solve a problem when there are many other interesting new problems that are out there to be solved.

In order to behave like a hacker, you need to believe that your time is precious. Think that it is your moral duty to share any information that you have from solving problems as well as solving any problem before you just give the solution away. This will help other hackers to be able to solve new problems that arise instead of having to solve ones that you may have answers to.

Remember, just because a problem has been solved does not mean that you shouldn't try and go back and find a new solution that might make solving that issue easier. This is never just one right solution to any given problem.

Often times we learn a lot from the problem that we didn't know before by studying the first solution to the problem. It is okay for you to believe that you can do better than the person who came up with the first solution. It is not okay however, to use artificial technical, legal, or even institutional barriers in order to prevent a good solution from being re-used therefore causing other people to have to re-invent the wheel.

You also do not need to feel obligated to hand over any of your creative product. You might want to remember that hackers are the ones that are going to give you the most respect as a hacker. It is perfectly okay for you to use your hacking skills in order to support your family or to get rich as long as you do not forget where your loyalties are to the art form of hacking as well as your fellow hackers who are the ones who are going to help you on your way up.

3.   Boredom and drudgery are evil: being that hackers are naturally creative; you should never get bored or have to drudge at work that is repetitive. This will cause you to not be able to solve new problems, which is the whole reason you're doing what you're doing!

Therefore, boredom and drudgery are not just unpleasant, but they are actually evil to a hacker.

In order to behave like a hacker, you're going to need to believe this enough to make sure that you do not fall into boredom. You also need to be able to spot when you have hit a wall so that you can find a way to get yourself off of it. You need to do this not only for yourself, but others as well.

Just like most things, there is an expectation to this rule. As a hacker, you will do things that are going to be repetitive or even boring to a normal observer. These are done as a mind-clearing exercises or for you to be able to acquire a skill that you have no experience in, or even to sharpen your skill in a certain area.

This type of "boredom" is perfectly okay because it is by choice. You should never be forced into a situation that is going to cause you to be bored and stifle your creativity.

4.   Freedom is good: as a hacker, you are most likely anti-authoritarian. (This does not have to be to the point that you do not respect any authority, however, for some hackers it does go this far).

When someone gives you an order that will spot you from solving a problem that you are fascinated by, it will generally cause you to fight harder to solve the problem.

As most authority minds think, they will find some sort of reason as to why it is stupid that you are attempting to solve this problem. Therefore, it is important that you try and fight this type of mindset so that you do not become smothered.

Remember that this does not mean that you are fighting all authority. As a hacker, you need to be able to accept some sort of authority so that you are able to get things that you want. This does not mean that you have to allow the authority to smother you and stop you from hacking.

To behave like a hacker, you need to develop an instinctive hostility to any censorship, use of force or deception, censorship or anything that is used to compel responsible adults. You need to be willing to act on that belief alone.

5.   Attitude is no substitute for competence: if you are going to be a hacker, you need to have some of these attitudes. However, copping an attitude alone is not going to make you a hacker any more than standing in a garage is going to make you a car.

To become a hacker, it is going to take practice, dedication, hard work, and intelligence from you.

Because of this, you are going to need to learn to distrust any attitude given to you and respect the competence of every kind. Hackers are not going to let some hacker want to be waste their time, however they will worship competence. Especially when that competence at hacking, but competence at anything is actually valued.

Competence is demanding skills that very few can master is especially good and competence at demanding skills that involve mental craft, concentration, and acuteness is the best.

If you are able to revere competence, you will then enjoy developing it in yourself. Hard work and dedication will become an intense play rather than drudgery. This attitude is vital to you becoming a hacker

Chapter 2: How to Think like a Hacker

In order to get into the mindset of a hacker, you first need to know how you are to think like a hacker.

A hacker is someone who finds the security flaws within a system and exploits them either for good in order to show someone where the holes are, or will use those holes in order to get all your sensitive data and essentially destroy your entire life.

1.   First, you need to be able to identify their exploits as well as any other information that will help you to create a footprint analysis. This is basically you getting as much information on your client as you possibly can.

You need to be able to consider the size of your target and any potential entry ways that you can use in order to get into their network as well as any security measures that are in place.

As a hacker, you need to think about the company names as well as their subsidiaries, phone numbers, domain names, and even IP addresses.

2.   Pay attention to back door entry points: this would be you looking for things like startup companies that are most likely going to have a weak security system since they are just starting out. This will be prevalent in companies that have recently been bought out by a larger company as well.

When you hack into these smaller companies, they may be able to provide you information for private networks that will lead you into a larger company's network as your next target.

3.   Connect to the listening UDP and TCP ports: when you do this, you are able to send out random data in order to determine what type of version of File Transfer protocol, mail server, or even web server that the company is using. There are many TCP and UDP servers that will send data in order to identify any running applications as a response to random data that has been sent. By doing this, you will be able to find the exploits by cross-referencing any data that you have found in a vulnerable database such as SecurityFocus.

4. Think about how you are going to gain access to your target: are you going to need a password and a user account in order to gain access to the network? Make sure that you are prepared. In having a username and password, you will be able to make a sneak attack into the network.

Once you have gotten into the network you will be able to take information from their website as well as be able to directly contact employees via phone. When doing this, you are able to pretend to be the help desk or even a tech from the IT department.

Most times, the employee will be completely unsuspecting and will give you any information that you are seeking because they honestly believe that you are from that department. Just make sure that it sounds authentic.

5. Take the username and password obtained and "Trojan" the system: now that you have a username and password of someone who actually works within the company, you are able to sneak into the company website unsuspected, much like the Greeks did with the Trojan Horse.

You are now able to replace software such as Notepad with a piece of Trojan code. This will allow you to become an administrator on the system and therefore you will have access to log on at a later date.

You will also automatically be added to the administrators group and have instant access to any information that is "admin only."

Chapter 3: How to Hack a Computer System

Hacking was used to help with gaining information about system for IT purposes when it was brought to the public's attention as something that was not all bad. It is now days that hacking has taken on a darker meaning thanks to those who use their skills for personal gain while hurting others.

When you look at the positive end of the hacking scale, there are multiple multimillion dollar companies that have hackers employed in their IT departments in order to help test the strength of their systems so that they know where they are most vulnerable and can beef up their security in order to help keep their companies safe. Due to being employed by a large company, hackers will only hack as far as they are allowed into the system and then help the company to fix the holes that they find. This help is what earns them the large salary that the companies pay them to help keep their information protected.

There are also hackers that work outside of the company that doe the same thing only they work with security consulting firms that the multimillion dollar companies hire in order to find the flaws in their security systems.

Before you begin to hack, there are steps that you need to follow in order to make sure that you are prepared for the experience of hacking that you will gain when you try and hack into a system. We have talked about these steps before in previous chapters, but they are worth going over again just to ensure that you are fully prepared when it comes to hacking into the system that you are granted access to.

Step One: Programming language is a necessity when it comes to hacking. As we've talked about earlier, there are is a variety of different programming languages that you can learn and it is best that you learn all of them so that you have a well-rounded knowledge of programming languages. It is vitally important that you know how a program speaks and works with the operating system that it is on. The more that you know, the easier that it will be for you to be able to gain access to the network.

Unix uses a C programming language and this teaches the memory how to work and knowing how this works is vitally important to learning how to hack into any system.

Python and Ruby are programming languages that are both very powerful programming languages that are used to automate a variety of tasks.

PHP and Perl is used for web applications and is a very reasonable choice for those who are in the hacking field.

If you are going to be scripting, you should be using Bash. This program easily manipulates the Unix and Linux systems therefore doing most of the job for you.

Assembly is the most basic language that your processor is going to understand. All programs can and will interpret assembly as it is the most basic language that any computer has. If you do not have a good knowledge of assembly, then you will never truly be able to exploit a program.

Step Two: you need to know your target. It is vitally important that you gather as much information as possible on the target that you are planning to hack. In getting this information you will need to be able to find the weak spots in their system. There is a chance that you're going to need to have different approaches in order to get into the system should you find that your initial approach is not the way to go. The more that you know about your target, the less chance that you'll find a surprise while you are hacking the system. When you gather information on your target it is known as enumeration.

Hacking:

Step One: You're going to want to use a *nix terminal for all your commands that you're going to be using when it comes to hacking. Cygwin is a good program that will actually emulate the *nix for those users who use Windows. If you do not have access to Cygwin, then it is best that you use Nmap which will run off WinPCap while you're still on windows even though you're not using Cygwin. However, the downside to Nmap is that it will run poorly on the Windows operating system because there is a lack of raw sockets.

When you're actually hacking, you're most likely going to want to consider using BSD or Linux as both of these systems are flexible no matter what type of system you are using. But, it is important to know that Linux will have more tools that are pre-installed and ultimately more useful to you when it comes to your hacking ventures.

Step Two: make sure that the machine you are using to hack is actually secured. You're going to need to make sure that you are protected before you go hacking into anyone else's system. If you are not secured, then there is a possibility that you are going to be traced and they will be able to get ahold of you and even file a lawsuit against you because they now know where you are.

If you're hacking a system that is a friend, family members, or a companies, make sure that you do not do so without the permission of the system's owner. The permission needs to ultimately be handwritten so that there are no repercussions that can come back on you.

If you do not feel comfortable attacking someone else's system, then you always have the option of attacking your own system in order to find your own securities flaws. In order to do this, you'll need to set up a virtual laboratory to hack.

Ultimately, it does not matter what you are trying to hack, if you do not have the permission of the administrator, it is illegal and you will get in trouble.

Step Three: you're going to want to make sure that you can reach the system in which you are trying to attack. You can use a ping utility tool in order to test and see if your target is active, however, the results from this cannot always be trusted. If you are using a ping utility tool, the biggest flaw you will find is that the system administrator will actually be able to turn their system off and therefore causing you to lose your target.

Step Four: you're going to need to run a scan of the ports on the system that you're trying to attack by using pOf or Nmap in order to check and see which ports are actually open on the machine. Along with telling you which ports are open, you'll also be able to see what type of firewall is being used as well as what kind of router is being used.

Knowing this type of information is going to help you to plot your course of action in attacking the system. In order to activate the OS detection using Nmap, you're going to use the -O switch.

Step Five: Ports such as those that use HTTP or FTP are going to more often than not be protected ports and are only going to become unsecure and discoverable when they are exploited.

Ports that are left open for LAN gaming such as TCP and UDP are often forgotten much like the Telnet ports.

Any ports that are open are usually evidence of a SSH (secure shell service) that is running on your target. Sometimes these ports can be forced open with brute force in order to allow you access to them.

Step Six: before you are able to gain access to most systems, there is a password that you're going to have to crack. You are able to use brute force in order to crack the password as one of the ways that you can try and get into a system. When you use brute force, your effort of trying every possible password contained within a pre-defined dictionary is put onto a software program and used to try and crack the password.

Being that users of any website or system are highly discouraged from using passwords that are weak and easy to crack, sometimes using brute force can take some time in trying to crack a password. However, there have been some major improvements to the brute force techniques in an effort to lower the time that it takes to crack a password.

You can also improve your cracking speed by using cracking algorithms. Many hashing algorithms can be weak and therefore are exploited in using their weakness in order to easily gain access to the system that you are trying to attack.

For example, if you have an MD5 algorithm and cut it in 1/4, you will then have a huge boost in the speed used to crack the password.

Graphics cards are also now being used as another sort of processor that you can gain access to. Gaining access to a graphics card is a thousand times faster than it is to crack a password or use an algorithm in order to attack the system.

It is highly advised that you do not try and attempted every possible password option when you are trying to access a machine remotely. If you're going to use this technique, then you're more than likely going to be detected due to the pollution of the system logs and it will take years to complete.

When you're using an IP address to access a proxy, you're going to need to have a rooted tablet as well as install a program called TCP scan. The TCP will have a signal that will upload and allow you to gain access to the secure site that you're trying to attack.

In the end, when you look at it, the easiest way to gain access to any system is to find a way that does not require you to have to crack a password.

Step Seven: if you're targeting a *nix machine, you're going to need to try and get the root privileges. When you're trying to gain access to a Windows system, you're going to need to get the administrator privileges.

If you want to see all the files on the system, you're going to need to have super-user privileges. Having super user privileges allows you to have an account that will give you access as a root user in the Linux or BSD systems.

Even if you're wanting to have access to the most basic kinds of files on a computer, you're going to need to have some kind of privileges that will allow you to see the files. So, no matter what, if you're wanting to see anything on a computer, you're going to need to have some sort of privileges that will allow you to see what is on the network. These privileges will come from the system administrator.

A system that uses a router will allow you to have access to the system by you using an admin account. The only reason that you would not be able to have access to it is if the router password has been changed by the router administrator. If you're using a Windows operating system, then you're going to have to have access to the administrator account.

Remember that if you gain access to the operating system, that does not mean that you will have access to everything that is on the operating system. In order to have access to everything, you're going to need to have a root account, super user account, or an administrator account.

Step Eight: there are ways that you can create a buffer overflow so that you can then use in order to give yourself super user status. The buffer overflow is what allows the memory to dump therefore giving you access to inject a code or in order to perform a task that is on a higher level then what you are authorized to do.

Software that is bugged usually has a setuid bit set in the unix system. This system allows a program to execute a task as if it were a different user.

Once again it is important that you get the administrators permission in writing before you begin to attack an insecure program on their operating system.

Step Nine: you worked hard to get into the system, you're going to want to make sure that you do not use up as much time getting back out. The moment that you have access to a system that is an SSH server, you will be able to create what is known as a back door so that you can gain access back to the system whenever you want without spending nearly as much time as you did the first time. A hacker that is experienced is more likely to have a back door in order to have a way in using complied software.

Step Ten: it is vitally important that you do not allow the system administrator to know that you got into their system and that it has been compromised. The way that you can ensure that they do not know is to not make any changes to the website or create more files than what you're going to need to create. You also should not create any additional users or you're going to instantly send up a red flag to the administrator.

If you are using a patched serve such as an SSHD server, you're going to need to code your password so that no one can log in using that password. If they happen to log in with that password, they will then have access that they should not have and they will have access to crucial information that you're most likely not going to want them to have access to.

When someone begins to try and log into the system, you need to get out immediately before you are caught. If caught, you're going to face some serious charges.

Chapter 4: How to Hack Wireless Networks

For this chapter, we are going to use different scenarios in order to help you better understand how to hack into different wireless networks.

Wireless networks are routers or any other way that a person or family gets WiFi in their home or business. These can usually be easily hacked because a lot of people do not change the password to the router from the original password that is given by the wireless provider.

It is a good idea to always change the password that is provided on the router that transmits data into the location in which it is located. This will help to make it harder for hackers to get into your WiFi therefore making it easier for them to get access to yourself.

Scenario 1: There is a computer that has no encryption on it which means that the network is wide open. Therefore, there is no isolation for the client and the network is considered to be unsafe to use and easy to hack.

Scenario 2: WEP is being used. There are several known attacks that exist and it will then make it easy to hack the network.

Scenario 3: The computer is not encrypted except for the isolation is enabled and a captive portal exists. With this type of wireless network, it is acceptable for a visitor to use the internet. Therefore, it should not be used for a company as it is still easy to be hacked.

Scenario 4: WPA/WPA2 is being used and a strong password has been put to use. The password has sixty characters, lower-case, upper-case, no dictionary words, and special characters in it. A hacker would not be able to crack the password with any computing power that we currently have. However, if the password is not changed every three months, there is a likelihood that a hacker will be able to figure out the password.

Scenario 5: WPA/WPA2, a weak password has been chosen. A hacker can now capture the authentication handshake and then make some attempts to crack it by using his own machine or even a "cloud" server. The server can then be compromised within a minute all the way up to a few hours.

Scenario 6: A company is using a WPA and a strong password that they change every day. But, the router that they are using in order to transmit WiFi has a static WPS pin that they are not able to change or even disable. Because WPS is enabled, this is very similar to having an open network. So, this network is considered to be unsafe and should not be used for business purposes.

Scenario 7: RADIUS is being used and the settings are weak when it comes to the wireless clients and the server. A hacker would be able to perform what is called a rouge AP attack and obtain the authentication handshake.
Should a weak password also be used, it can be captured and user accounts will be at risk as well as the network being compromised. It is important for each person on this type of network to have their own password that is tied directly to the domain. This means that the hacker will not be able to hack the wireless network as well as the domain.

Scenario 8: The company is using WPA/WPA2, as well as a strong password that is changed every day. The WPS is disabled and the administrator's computer is kept up to date.
But, the router has not been updated since being installed and it contains odays (unknown vulnerabilities) that will allow a hacker to be able to conduct a CSRF attack. This is done by a persistent threat and the following can happen:

-    The router will be compromised

-    The hacker will be able to send targeted emails within the system administrators system that will cause it to appear like it is being sent from the router vender. This will also inform the system administrator to log into the router and check the email by clicking a link within the email after they have logged in.

-    The link will then redirect the administrator to a page that will change the routers settings or simply steal the password.

It is also possible for a hacker to be able to get into a system because an employee has shared the password to the system unknowingly with a hacker and then makes the system compromised. This can also happen knowingly.

Or, if an employee's phone or computer is compromised, then the wireless network password is compromised as well.

You should have a strict ACLs from the wireless to any segment that is wired. There should also be strict ACLs to any server that is going to hold sensitive information.

Chapter 5: How to Crack Passwords

Passwords are going to be the easiest way to get into someone's computer. However, even though you have to be highly skilled in order to get a password correct the first time.

But, there other ways that you are able to go about hacking into someone's system by using their password. These techniques are not always going to be effective and some of them are not going to work period.

Do not put all your faith in thinking that you're going to hack someone's password. Some passwords are not going to be able to be hacked because of how everyone is constantly told that they need to make sure that they have strong passwords in order to make sure that they are not hacked.

1.   Dictionary Hack: this is when you use actual dictionary words in order to try and hack someone's password. This is used by trying to determine different passphrases and using a trial and error method.

This works much like a normal dictionary; however, it is just a simplified file that contains unusual words that many people are going to place inside of their password. This makes it easy to hack their password. However, a tough password will always beat this attack.

Dictionary Attack

- Most people use real words as passwords
- Try all dictionary words before trying a brute force attack
- Makes the attack much faster

2.   Brute Force Attack: the motto for the brute force attack is to crack passwords. A brute force attack will try every possible combination in order to crack the password.

With people being smarter as technology changes, the growing size of passwords is making it hard for brute force to be able to crack the passwords.

This is very similar to the dictionary attack but is basically an upgraded version.

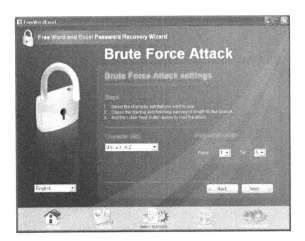

3.   Phishing: this is by far the easiest method that you can use as a hacker. Phishing asks a user for its password in a unique and different way. As the hacker, you are able to create fake emails, apps, pages and other things that are going to ask you to log in with your id and password. At the point in time that you have logged in, your passwords are instantly transmitted into the hacker's computer for them to be able to access your sensitive data.

4.   Viruses, Trojans, and other Malware: a virus is a program that a hacker can develop in order to destroy their intended target. These worms and viruses can get into a user's system and therefore give the hacker full use of the system. At this point in time, a hacker has full use of the network or machine and can spread the virus through emails or other hidden applications.

5.   Shoulder Surfing: this is the practice of spying on the user of any electronic device in order to obtain personal information. This is usually found in eye catching notes that are stuck in front of your monitor that keep asking you to login.

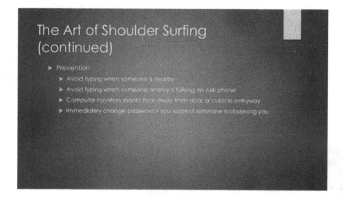

6.   Port Scan Attack: this is a technique that is used in order to find the weakness on any given server. Normally it is used by those who are responsible for security in order to find vulnerabilities within the system.

Port Scan Attacks are used to send messages to a port while waiting for a response. The data that is received from the open port is then an invitation for a hacker to get into your server.

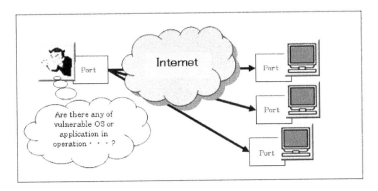

Chapter 6: How to Protect Yourself from Hackers

Some people use their hacking skills to gain access to information that they are able to use to harm others. Information that is taken is your personal information like your social security, address, or credit card numbers. It does not take a lot of information in order to someone to gain access to your entire identity. As long as they have a few key pieces of information then they can pass themselves off as you and ultimately ruin your life. the hackers that do this are out to help only themselves at the cost of anyone that it takes. As long as the information helps them further themselves enough that they are able to go on hacking into the next person's life.

However, you are able to avoid situations like this by doing some small things that most people do not think about when it comes to helping them save their identity. Below are a few of these steps that can help you to protect yourselves a little more against hackers who are out to harm you and your family.

off the WiFi and Bluetooth on your phone. Keeping on these features allows hackers to have easy access to your phone.

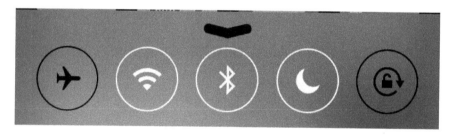

When you keep the WiFi and Bluetooth on all the time, hackers have access to see what networks you have been connected to and be able to create a fake network with the same name so that they are able to trick your phone into connecting to a device because it believes that device is actually the network that you have authorized to have access to your phone.

At the point in time that your phone is now connected to the device of the hacker's choosing, they are able to gain access to your data that is stored there as well as spy on what information that you put into your phone. Not only that, but they are able to place malware on your phone so that you can never trace the fact that they were in your phone.

Therefore, you should turn your Bluetooth and WiFi off when you are not using it so that you are able to protect your phone just a little bit more.

Another way you can protect yourself is to never use the one password. When you use one password, you make it too easy for yourself to be hacked and they are exposed all the time because of how limited the security is into whatever the hacker wants access to. So, in order to protect yourself, use a two-step authentication so that if your password is entered in wrong, it will then ask you for a second password in order to verify that you are who you say you are.

A lot of social media sites and even email services now are able to offer extra protection. The two-step authentication is essentially a temporary password that gives you access to what a hacker is trying to get into.

When you join sites such as LinkedIn, Twitter, or Google, you are asked to enter a code each time you even attempt to log into your account from a new device. This code is sent to whatever email or phone number you have on file for the account. Should you change your email or phone and not change it with your account, you will then not be able to access your account.

Although someone may be able to get a hold of your password, it is highly unlikely that they are going to have access to your phone's messages as well in order to get the verification code that they need.

For websites that you access containing sensitive information such as your email or your bank account, you should use a passphrase that is both unique and long. An example would be +HISpl@tinumDr@gonBreathsfire.

When you are getting into something that does not contain some of your sensitive data, you can then save your password on the password manager that is on your computer so that you do not have to remember the password.

The most important thing for you to remember is that when you use the password manager, it encrypts any passwords that are stored on your device. Programs such as Password Safe and LastPass will do this for you so that your passwords are still protected.

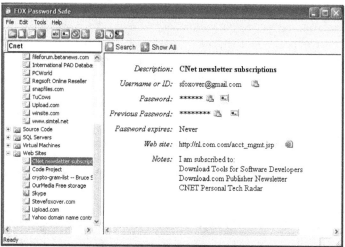

If you are using one password for everything, it acts like a master password that will unlock everything and once a hacker has access to one password, they will be able to gain access to any website that you have ever gotten on.

It is also a good idea for you to change your passwords more than once a year in order to keep your accounts up to date.

Whie you are browsing the web, make sure that you are using HTTPS. The program HTTPS Everywhere is a tool that encrypts all the information that is transmitted or received by your browser when you visit multiple websites.

If there is no s at the end of the HTTP in the address bar of the website that you are visiting, then anyone can view what you are currently viewing.

When you are setting up your home WiFi, you need to set it up with a password. Many routers come with a sticker on the side of the box that will give you access to that specific network. Make sure that you change it! Do not stay with the default password because it is entirely too easy to be hacked for someone to be able to gain access to your network.

Also, when the machine asks what kind of security encryption you want, it is best to choose WPA-2.

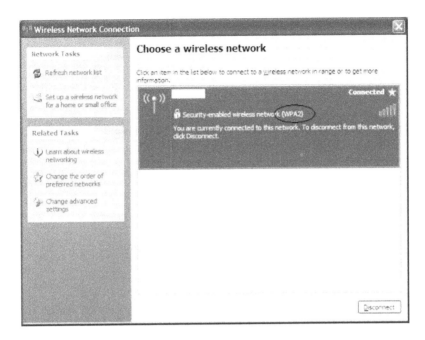

It is wise to attempt and try and voice WEP and WPA at all costs. The encryptions actually have a flaw that will give up the password to your network within a few seconds.

At the time that your home router is set up, it will ask you if you want to hide the SSID. When you click yes, your WiFi will be hid from others, but it will force your devices to constantly search for the network that they are connected to. Your devices will connect, but in the time that is spent scanning for the network, it will open up your device to connecting to a strange network.

Now days there are devices such as a smart fridge, oven, and even washer and dryer. These devices connect to the internet and give you different options that the original designs don't.

But, the companies that are putting out these devices are still working out the kinks in them.

While tech companies rush around and just slap WI-FI connectivity on everything, they are skipping the important things such as privacy and safety of their devices users.

An important example of this is when a hacker hijacked a baby monitor and said some very foul mouthed things over the device.

Hacker Stanislav says that even though you are told things are secure with your device, they might not be.

Ultimately, security over your devices is up to you in order to protect yourself and those you love.

Other ways to keep yourself protected are to keep your firewall turned on. Your firewall helps keep hackers out of your computer. Some operating systems already come with a firewall that you can use or you can purchase a program with a firewall.

Always keep your antivirus software updated. Designed to prevent malicious software from embedding in your computer, antivirus programs help to protect your computer. At any point in time, when the program detects a virus or a worm, it works to remove the threat. Virus' can gain access to your computer through hackers placing them there in order to spy on you.

Antispyware technology needs to be kept updated as well. Just as it sounds, spyware allows someone to be able to see all activity that is done on a computer. Some spyware actually collects data without your consent and then produces unwanted ads popping up on your web browser.

Outdated operating systems actually make it slightly easier for a hacker to enter your computer. With each new update, the security on a computer gets just a little better due to all the flaws that were found and fixed between updates. Leaving your system without these updates can give a hacker access to your machine.

Hackers can also get into your system through your email. Never open an email that is from someone you do not know. These emails can contain malicious code from hackers who are attempting to gain access to multiple machines in order to get information that they want.

Turn off your computer when you're not using it. Even though it is easier to just leave your computer up so that it is easily accessed, spyware and virus' still have access to your computer and still allow hackers to get into your computer without you knowing.

Chapter Seven: Techniques Used by Hackers

So far in this book you have learned how to hack different systems as well as how to get into the mindset of a hacker. However, just like anything out there, there are techniques that you can use in order to be a more effective hacker.

1. Anonymity: Hackers don't want you knowing that they got into your system. In doing this, they are going to make sure that they do anything that they can in order to not leave a trace. In doing this, they will use
- Proxies or secured tunnels
- Software that will hide their IP address
- Will use other people's usernames and passwords without using his own
- Programming that is written in C
- Or a telnet that will hide him and his task execution.

2. Getting Out: Any good hacker is going to make sure that they do not leave any trace on your computer so that you never know they were there. In the process of getting out the hacker is going to leave all your files alone, however, he is going to leave a "backdoor" open so that he is able to get back into your computer at a later date.

3. Gather information about the target: When hacking someone, it is important to get as much information on them as you possibly can. In doing this, you're going to want information such as:
- Their IP address
- Telnet or Tracert in order to look at the pings of when someone is on the computer
- And be resourceful. Find out as much about your target as you possibly can get.

4. Log the keystrokes: as a hacker, you are able to use programs that will review every keystroke that someone has made on their computer and that alone can reveal a person's identity.

5. Go for passwords: when trying to hack passwords, it is best to try and go with the simple algorithms that create a combination of letters, symbols, and numbers. This is a trial and error method. You'll need to make well educated guesses and use dictionary attacks so that you can generate every possible combination of the password.

6. Leave a virus: this is a simple way to get back into a computer. Leaving a virus can be done by simply sending out an email or instant message to any potiental victims.

7. Gain entry through a backdoor: this is extremely similar to hacking a password. There are many hackers who develop codes and programs that will look for defenseless pathways into networks as a way to enter the network without ever having to use a password.

8. Spy on email: this is a program that can be used so that you can interrupt and read emails.

9. Make zombie computers: this is when a computer is used by a hacker to place DDoS attacks and send out spam emails. If an innocent user clicks on the link that you send out, it will open up a connection between your computer and his.

10. Make sure that you have a firewall up so that you have restricted access to any personal information that may go outside of your computer.

11. Use a proxy server: when you decide to use the computer, make sure that you target proxy servers.

12.   Use search engines: this will help you to find the tools that you need in order to hack a system. From here, you can download the tools that you need in order to target a specific computer.

13.   Leave a file or two on the computer: this will allow you to gain easy access back into the computer at a later date. You can leave files such as Net cat in order to gain access again.

CHAPTER EIGHT: PURSUING A CAREER IN ETHICAL HACKING

Not all hackers are hackers who are going to be hacking into a system in order to gain access to your personal information. In fact, there are several very famous hackers that have come out of history that have given us the technology that we currently have. Three that come to mind are Steve Wozniak, Steve Jobs, and Captain Crunch.

These very well-known men began their career hacking and then have given us some of the technology that we know and enjoy today. All they did was take the knowledge that they had and applied it to technology and found new ways to create things.

In order to start your career as an ethical hacker, it is wise that you have some sort of computer science degree that will allow you to do this. Many big companies are hiring hackers to find the flaws in their systems so that they are able to keep their company secrets, secrets.

You can also use your hacking skills to be able to make your own technology like Wozniak and Jobs did. You are able to create programs and computers or whatever it is you are wanting to create in order to help people protect themselves from hackers.

If you are wanting to go to a company and work for them, then you are going to need to find the companies that are hiring people for their IT teams. You will be doing more than finding the security flaws in their systems, but it will put you in a step in the right direction.

It is important for you to remember that hacking is illegal unless it is done ethically. Here are some of the ways that hackers are punished if they are caught.

In India if you are found tampering with a computer source document which includes the destruction, concealment or event he alteration of the documents source code will end up getting the hacker at least three years in prison or a fine of 20000 rupees.

Also in India, if you are found just having hacked into a website or various other sources, you will be imprisoned for up to three years and possibly get a fine of 50000 rupees.

The Netherlands defines hacking as an intruding an automated work or part thereof with intention against the law. Intrusion would be considered defeating any security measures, false signals or false cryptographic keys, using stolen usernames or passwords. Any of these can get you at least one-year imprisonment along with a fine of the fourth category.

The United States prohibits any unauthorized use or damage of a protected computer. A protected computer would be a computer that is used by a financial institute or the US Government.

The computer can also be used in affecting interstate or foreign commerce or even communication. The computer does not have to be located in the United States if it is used for any type of interstate or foreign commerce.

The maximum imprisonment can be one year in a federal prison or a fine that is not more than $5,000.

Chapter Nine: Wozniak and Jobs

As mentioned in the previous chapter, Wozniak and Jobs used hacking in order to help improve technology. In this chapter, you are going to learn how they were able to do this.

Just like in a previous chapter, Jobs and Wozniak used a popular way of hacking in order to break into different computers.
Even though they used their hacking for good, what they were doing was still illegal!

Back in the 60s the term hacker was used to describe someone who was an expert at programming. As the years went on and more people got into hacking, the skills used in order to gain access to a system have gone from being "completely innocent" to having people who use it for illegal activity on the computer. Either way you look at it, the ones who use their skills to program a computer and make it better, or the ones who use their skills in order to gain access to a person's private information, they are both skilled individuals. Some of the biggest names in technology today started out "hacking" back in the beginning days of computers.

At the Computer History Museum in California, there is a device on display called a Blue Box. This box was used to interrupt phone signals and was invented by two hackers that are extremely well known today – Steve Jobs and Steve Wozniak.

As stated, the Blue Box was used to interrupt phone signals. It was a hacking activity that is known as phone phreaking.

Today, phone calls are a series of connections that place you through to who you wish to talk to. Back in the beginning, this was done by a human operator who would help you get through to the person you wanted to speak with. When the automatic exchanges came into place, they route your call to its destination by communicating with one another. The automatic exchanges use a series of audible tones known as signaling which came around in the 60s and 70s.

The tones that phones used proved to be the weak spot that hackers exploited.

The blue box emulates the signaling tones used by telephone exchanges. When these tones are played through a speaker that is connected to the phone's handset, the automatic exchanges are fooled into believing that they are receiving a signal. Anything became possible once the hacker understood all the signaling tones that were used.

A hacker could figure out how a call was routed by billing the processes, overriding the charging, and this would help them to overcome any blocking restrictions that a phone company had put in place. In the early 1970s this is what Jobs and Wozniak designed and began to sell. Using false names, (Berkeley Blue and Oaf Tobar), Jobs and Wozniak entered into the illegal world of Phone Phreaker.

Wozniak and Jobs started with Phone Preakering because they were interested in the challenge it gave them to take something apart and figure out how it works, and then find ways around it. By the time that they did figure it out, they also figured out that they could make money off of it, and that is when they began the illegal action of selling their work.

Now motivated by the new technical challenges that were coming out with the advancement of technology, Wozniak and Jobs abandoned their life of crime and moved on to different challenges. In an interview with Jobs, he claimed that if it hadn't been for the Blue Boxes that he and Wozniak experimented on, Apple would not exist today.

Blue Boxes became extinct when the telephone companies began to adopt an out of band signal that would spate and dedicate the connections that were used for exchange to exchange any communication.

By today's definition, Wozniak and Jobs would be considered hackers. But, were they really hackers or were they just skilled programmers? The line is thin in deciphering which side they fell on. They did know that they were engaging in illegal activities with their Blue Box. Is the only reason that they are not considered hackers because they are now a household name thanks to creating Apple?

On the other hand, things could have turned out very differently for Wozniak and Jobs. Due to all the hacks that have happened within the government now days, their Blue Boxes and other hacking antics would be far less likely to just be dismissed as harmless rebellion thanks to people feeling more sensitive to our privacy and communications. In fact, it is very possible that if Wozniak and Jobs had continued with their illegal activities, they would have ended up serving time.

But, since they learned a lot thanks to the use of their blue boxes. Without having dabbled in the darker side of hacking, Wozniak and Jobs would have never created the worldwide company that we all know and enjoy today.

Conclusion

Thank you again for downloading this book! We greatly appreciate it.

I hope this book was able to help you to gain some knowledge on what it means to be a hacker as well as how you can hack a wireless network and a computer. Not only that, but how you can be able to crack passwords in order to get into different systems.

The next step is to further your knowledge and try and hack into a computer system or wireless network.

Please remember that hacking is illegal and that it should not be done! If you are going to attempt to hack into any system, have the system administrator's permission before you even begin to formulate your plan on how you are going to expose their weaknesses.

Finally, if you enjoyed this book, then I'd like to ask you for a favor, would you be kind enough to leave a review for this book on Amazon? It'd be greatly appreciated!

www.ingramcontent.com/pod-product-compliance
Lightning Source LLC
Chambersburg PA
CBHW060934050326
40689CB00013B/3094